# THE LAW AND CIVICS READING AND WRITING INSTITUTE (LCRWI)

**GENERAL EDUCATION, TRAINING, AND RECRUITMENT**

# THE LAW AND CIVICS READING AND WRITING INSTITUTE (LCRWI)

## GENERAL EDUCATION, TRAINING, AND RECRUITMENT

*An Introductory Course Workbook
On Child Development Theories:*

*Educating Black Male Infants, Toddlers,
Preschoolers and Children*

## Dr. STANLEY HOWARD

*Co-Facilitators
Glodean Champion and Johnny Holmes II*

G-Course Series:
Human and Child Development (Theory Building)

Course G-101
Development Theories:
Black Male Infants, Toddlers, Preschoolers and Children

The Law and Civics Reading and Writing Institute (LCRWI) General Education, Training, and Recruitment Student Guide: An Introductory Course Workbook on Child Development Theories: Educating Black Male Infants, Toddlers, Preschoolers, and Children

COPYRIGHT© 2015 by Stanley Howard PhD.

Published by Anointed Life Publishing Company, Phoenix, Arizona
Published under the auspices of the Law and Civics Reading and Writing Institute

No part of this book may be reproduced or transmitted in any form or by any means, electronic or mechanical, including photocopying, recording, or any information storage retrieval system, without prior permission in writing from the publisher.

Queries regarding rights and permissions may be addressed to:
The Law and Civics Institute
PO Box 43046
Chicago, IL 60643-9998
info@LCRWI.org

Manufactured in the United States of America

Publisher's Cataloging-In-Publication Data
(Prepared by The Donohue Group, Inc.)

Howard, Stanley, 1955-
*Righting America's Wrongs: Student Guide: An Introductory Course Workbook on Child Development Theories: Educating Black Male Infants, Toddlers, Preschoolers, and Children*/Stanley Howard, Ph.D.

    Pages: illustrations; cm

ISBN: #       Softcover       978-0-9967582-0-8

1. African American boys—Education (Early childhood)—Workbook

To arrange to receive mentor education and training, or teacher professional development from this workbook, please send email to info@LCRWI.org

www.anointedlifepublishing.com

## Contents

Acknowledgements ......................................................................................... vii

About the Author ............................................................................................ viii

About the Co-Facilitators ................................................................................. ix

About the Education Think Tank ...................................................................... xi

Chapter 1 The Law and Civics Reading and Writing Institute ............................ 1

Chapter 2 The Law of Manhood Healing and Empathic Development .............. 9

Chapter 3 The Law of Maternal Health and Well-Being .................................. 15

Chapter 4 The Law of Fathers, 'Surrogate Fathers,' and Honorable Men ........ 23

Chapter 5 The Law of Social, Emotional, and Cognitive Development and Learning ......... 29

Chapter 6 The Law of the Rights of Black Male Children ................................ 35

Chapter 7 What is a Quality Education? ......................................................... 41

Course Evaluation .......................................................................................... 45

# Acknowledgements

We would like to thank Anita Howard for sharing her extensive knowledge as a teacher, educator, researcher, and development practitioner in the creation of this workbook. The workbook would not have been produced without her expert contributions and generous guidance.

We would like to also acknowledge the creative contributions to the workbook from Legacy Board members and Level-Four-Seeking Honorable Men of the Law and Civics Reading and Writing Institute: Gerald Deals, Gregory Washington and Michael Akanni. We particularly wish to thank them for their assistance in conducting research and brainstorming.

Thanks also for the advice, feedback, and general support of Dr. Ellen Hall, Dr. Iheoma I. Thompson, Dr. Susan Sarver, Dr. Jerry Weems, Dr. Michael Toney, Michelle and Joshua Dubois, Nana B. Ofori-atta, Dr. Willie Austin, Sharon Ritchie, Eric Grimes, Nancy Rosenow, Dr. Waldo Johnson, Carolyn and Keith Chambers, Michael and Sherry Kaufman, and Angela Fowler.

A special thanks to the many teachers and mentors who have hosted us through the years in their classrooms, youth centers, and boys and young men organizations. We are especially indebted to the Law and Civics Teacher Research Advisory Council for their participation in our Conversations with Master Teachers 2015-Series.

## About the Author

Dr. Stanley Howard is the founder and president of the solutions-based, education think tank: Law and Civics Reading and Writing Institute (LCRWI). The mission of LCRWI is to conduct empirical research and application on how children develop and learn. He has a PhD in political science, specializing in civil rights, civil liberties, and U.S. constitutional law. Over the past five years, he has cross-pollinated the study of political science with the fields of early childhood development and learning. This route has opened new and exciting research vistas through combining and exploring the cutting-edge research currently conducted in the fields of neuroscience, bio-development, culture, economics, multiple intelligences, and environment-based learning. By aggregating these fields of study under the auspices of the Institute, he is developing a model of early child development that promises evidence-based and common sense solutions that will effectively close the achievement and opportunity gaps experienced in early childhood schools, classrooms, child care centers, and teacher conferences around the nation. His theory-building research and application agenda over the next two years includes the impact of ecology and culture on 'whole child' development and learning of low-income and low-resourced American children of color; the human and civil rights of children, and the developmental benefits of providing children of color a civic education in their early years. Many of these topics are addressed in this course and workbook.

In collaboration with Dr. Howard, Glodean Champion and John Holmes, II also contributed to the creation of this workbook. They are certified facilitators at the Institute.

## About the Co-Facilitators

**G**lodean Champion *is the supervisor of the International Academic and Cultural Exchange Division of the Law and Civics Reading and Writing Institute. Her research agenda at the Institute addresses child development and learning in different ecological, cultural, and civic contexts. Her work has taken her to Africa, Europe, and other parts of the world. As a professor of writing, she has taught at numerous colleges in the United States. Champion is also a celebrated photographer and author.*

**J**ohnny Holmes, II *is supervisor of male mentoring at the Law and Civics Reading and Writing Institute. In that capacity, he conducts interdisciplinary research on how children develop and learn, specializing in 0-3 brain development. He supervises LCRWI's male mentors in program development, implementation and evaluation for early childhood through middle school. As a youth counselor and community activist for over 18 years, Holmes has been guided by Frederick Douglas' observation that "It is easier to build strong children, than to repair broken men." Holmes is the author of the heralded book, <u>Thy Kingdom Come: The Effects of Praise and Worship</u>.*

## About The Education Think Tank

### Mission

The Law and Civics Reading and Writing Institute (LCRWI) is a solution-based education think tank that conducts multi-disciplinary research, implementation, evaluation and advocacy, on the development and learning of children, especially at-risk children from birth through adolescence. Our objective is to build a reputation among educational institutions, community stakeholders, civic groups, faith-based groups, and policymakers as the most rigorous, knowledgeable, and reliable education think tank in the United States and the world.

Note: Another important goal of the Institute is to share its research discoveries with all stakeholders. However, community stakeholders, like many of you taking the course, are especially important to the work of the think tank, since you are closest to the children, families and communities we seek to serve.

### How to Use This Guide/Chapter Organization

This student guide is a companion for *Righting America's Wrongs: A Best Practices Manual for Educating Black Male Youth* by Dr. Stanley Howard. It is designed with two other purposes in mind. First, it should be seen by adult learners in the courses, as a personal journal that will not only deliver important information on the human development of vulnerable children in their early years, but also as a problem solving learning tool to help facilitate the required service learning part of the course. For example, sections such as "What Do You Think," "Community Service Learning," "Solutions that Solve," and the "Glossaries" both General and LCRWI are intentionally designed to engender reflection, and action-oriented community engagement. Secondly, the guide was created to provide assistance to teachers, trainers, facilitators, and adjunct faculty at the Law and Civics Reading and Writing Institute.

When using the guide, adult learners should thoughtfully reflect on each subject area presented in the chapters. Each chapter covers a research-grounded topic that is seen as critical to providing Black male children, in their early years, with the kinds of healthy learning environments and nurturing relationships they need to successfully grow and development. However, to achieve this goal, child care professionals must work to close the gap between what we in fact scientifically know about how children develop and learn, and how we implement the knowledge, i.e., what we actually do with them in our homes, day cares, and classrooms. In the book's last chapter (Chapter 7), adult learners are asked to aggregate their research-based information, knowledge, and reflection as an in-service provider to create their very own personal civic and scientific plan to build community education think tanks that are seamlessly connected to high-quality pre-k thru eighth grade community schools, to serve low-income and low-resourced children in urban and rural America.

The course itself is grounded in human and child development theories and practices. It specifically addresses issues of how can we, as a society, better educate Black boys in their early years of development and learning. The primary groups targeted to help discover answers to this question are parents, teachers, mentors, human services workers, community activists, and policy makers. One of the many unique instructional features of the course is how it has situated this question in a gender context. In other words, the workbook has a number of brainstorming and class activities based on how both men and women view the issue of educating Black males in their early years, and the roles they might play separately and together in achieving this desired goal.

**Course Title:**
*G-101: Development Theories: Black Male Infants, Toddlers, Preschoolers and Children*

**Course Description:**
This research-based general education and training course is the first in a sequence of courses designed specifically for child care workers in the fields of education, social welfare, and human services charged with successfully responding to issues of child poverty, child abuse and neglect, child and youth development, and children's rights. It is also created for ordinary women and men in American communities, i.e., mothers, fathers, uncles and aunties seeking scientific and commonsense answers to how our society can create educational institutions of hope that nurture resilience, self-esteem, and confidence in vulnerable children of color.

This course will engage this and related issues by examining human and child development theories. More specifically, it will engage adult learners in theory building that will support males in their early years of development and learning (birth to eight years of age) and especially males of color. Students will engage these theories because they help development practitioners form a profile of what children can do at various ages, and how they should respond based on this knowledge. Students will also be presented with the very latest research in brain development, e.g., zero to age three--a "critical period of brain development," and the impact of early environments on employment and other human skills development. The course especially highlights development and learning from the perspective of young Black male children in America. A major part of our inquiry will be on the learning and development of these children from Black boyhood to manhood in the context of American Democracy. We will address the subjects of boyhood and manhood from ethnic, racial, gender, economic, cultural and other fields of study.

As is the case with all courses in the general education theory sequence, this education and training course has a service learning/fieldwork component that requires students to personally and collectively brainstorm "on the ground" family and community educational issues. Using their own ideas and reflections generated by the information they have received, adult learners will make their own personal and collective research contributions to the process of discovering and building promising development theories that have practical and promising application in low-resourced and marginalized American communities. The service learning question that students are required to address is: what are the possible educational benefits to disadvantaged children, families, and communities of creating community think tanks that are seamlessly connected to community schools.

**Teaching Approach:**
Using a cooperative learning format, where adults learners are seen as both consumers and creators of knowledge, the course will review theories of human and child development, critique the prevailing education model on how children (especially males) develop and learn, and collectively discuss the educational, ethnic/racial, social, moral, economic, and civic implications of this knowledge from the developmental and learning needs of Black male infants, toddlers, preschoolers, and children in the nation. They will be introduced to the eco-cultural model that situates child development in the various environments in which children actually live and play. This model also challenges the dominant and exclusionary "one size fits all" developmental perspective, and offers new ways of thinking about how to successfully educate undervalued and silenced children of color. The course will also present adult learners with the research-based idea that all children are born with innate curiosity, imagination, creativity, resilience, and problem-solving potential. Students will be asked to consider the validity of this proposition from the perspective of African American child rearing and learning, cultural practices, and its implications for determining their role in successfully educating Black male children.

**Course Objectives / Topics for Discussion:**
- The Human Brain
    - Building from the bottom up
    - The critical period of brain development (0-3)
    - The "male brain"
- What is "manhood?"
- What is a man's civic responsibility (to a woman/wife, children, family, and community)?
- Exploring the benefits of role modeling
- Considering the possibility of viable and wholesome educational systems
- Understanding the impact of gender equality on health, safety and well-being
- Discussion: Where are the honorable men?
- The impact of maternal depression and stress
    - Pregnancy and female hormones
- What are the responsibilities of honorable men of vision?
- What is a father?
    - Must a father be "biological?"
    - Can a mother be a father and teach a boy how to be a man?
- The male brain
    - Black boys and ADHD
- What is the scientific mind?

- Understanding learned "victimization"
- Exploring Eric Erickson's psycho-social stages of development
- Review of the impacts of addictions to:
  - Alcohol
  - Cigarettes
  - Drugs
  - Etc.
- Children of color and the American civic story
- The Civil Rights Movement vs. the human rights fight on
  - Children
  - The 1st Amendment
  - The United Nations
- Exploring the importance of trust relationships
- The "Quality Education" -- what does it look like? Can it ever exist?
- Is critical thinking disappearing from the classroom?
- How do we get our children to think and have confidence that their opinions matter?

Note: These topics are found in LCRWI's book, *Righting America's Wrongs: A Best Practices Manual for Educating Black Male Youth*, which is the primary source used in the course.

**Course Requirements:**

Because the course is designed on cooperative learning principles and practices, students are expected to engage lecturers and one another on the many topics presented. Also as mentioned above, keep in mind that students are seen as both consumers and creators of knowledge. Students will be assessed on the quality of workbook assignments (35pts); class participation (15pts); and the community service learning project (50pt).

**Course Lecturers:**
Dr. Stanley Howard, Ms. Glodean Champion, and Mr. Johnny Holmes, II

**Visiting Scholars and Guest Lecturers:** (TBA)

**Course Required Texts:**
1. Howard, Stanley. *Righting America's Wrongs: A Best Practices Manual for Educating Black Male Youth*. Illinois. Law and Civics Publishing: 2014
2. Howard, Stanley. *An Introductory Workbook: Educating Black Males in Their Early Years* (Human and Child Development). Arizona. Anointed Life Publishing: 2015

# Chapter 1

# The Law and Civics Reading and Writing Institute

**Did You Know?**

- Children as young as preschool will receive many cognitive and moral self-development benefits from a civic-engagement curriculum that teaches them the interrelationship between their family, school, community, nation, and world.
- When we recognize a child's right to be civically engaged, we are simultaneously preparing him to become a civically empowered adult.
- During the Civil Rights Movement, Black children, some as young as 9 years old, were credited with "saving" the movement in some of its darkest hours.
- In many elite private schools, children in early childhood receive a comprehensive civic education.

**Myth or Science:**

*Topic: The Expulsion of Black Male Preschoolers*

**Myth:** Black male preschoolers are suspended and expelled at a higher rate than their white and Asian counterparts because their classroom behavior is more unruly.

**Science:** According to a study by early childhood researchers Barbarin and Crawford, Black male preschoolers are suspended and expelled more often; mainly because their behaviors are stigmatized more than the behaviors of other children.

**What Do You Think?**

- Reflect on "Tabula Rasa" from the view of educating young children.
- Reflect on some of the benefits Black males in early childhood would receive from a civic education.
- How can an understanding of the connections between politics and economics assist in the education of children in their early years?
- Should early childhood educators receive a "heart and mind" civic education? Why? Why not?

**Student Assignments:**

**Readings:**

- Barbarin, A. Oscar. "*Halting African American Boys' Progression From Pre-k to Prison: What Families, Schools, and Communities Can Do!*" The Community American Journal of Orthopsychiatry, vol. 80, No1, 81-88. 2010
- Howard, Dr. Stanley. *Righting America's Wrongs: A Best Practices Manual For Educating Black Male Youth*. Illinois. Law and Civics Publishing: 2014
- Kaufman, Michael. *Learning Together: The Law, Politics, Economics, Pedagogy, and Neuroscience of Early Childhood Education*. (Chapters 1 and 2) Maryland. Rowman & Littlefield: 2015

**Videos:**

- Ea, Prince. **(**2014, Sep. 29). *Can We Auto-Correct Humanity?* https://youtube/dRl8EIhrQjQ
- Facebook (2013, June, 7). *Boulder Colorado Journey School Children and Civic-engagement.*
  https://vimeo.com/66934951
- Sssirob. (2009, Nov. 2). *President Franklin Delano Roosevelt Second Bill of Rights*. https://www.youtube.com/watch?v=effDfpKYcV0
- White. (2013, Apr. 23). *Children March and Jailed.* https://www.youtube.com/watch?v=DKXFSvrlyWc

# Chapter 1
## The Law and Civics Reading and Writing Institute

**Solutions That Solve:**

Below are ten research-based rights of the Black male child that were proposed and adopted by the Law and Civics Reading and Writing Institute. They were adopted to underscore the importance of schools, families, communities, and policy makers honoring and respecting the human and civil rights of Black boys to self-determination and self-expression in their early years. From the view of "Solutions That Solve," reflect on these rights in the context of the civic principles that are presented in this chapter:

Black males have:

1. The right to have their human rights and civil rights honored, respected, nurtured, and protected.
2. The right to have their curiosity, imagination, and creativity honored, respected, nurtured, and protected.
3. The right to be problem solvers.
4. The right to healthy social emotional development, both in and out of the classroom.
5. The right to loving, caring, trusting, and nurturing relationships with teachers.
6. The right to a happy and stress-free childhood and boyhood.
7. The right to have their culture honored, respected, and nurtured.
8. The right to explore, discover, and learn with nature.
9. The right to develop trusting inter-generational relationships with caring adults.
10. The right to develop trusting relationships with honorable men who are committed to form a "circle of protection" to guide them into manhood.

**In-Class Activity (TBA):**

**Service Learning (Community Field Work):**

A group of community education stakeholders are considering placing civic curricula in the schools in your community for K-3 children. They have solicited your research-based opinion on the developmental value that such a program would provide? Reflect on the response you would provide and offer your argument below.

**Glossary (General):**

*Achievement gap*—A persistent, measurable, educational disparity between two groups of students-usually differing by race, socioeconomic status, and or gender.

*Democracy*—A system of government by the whole population of all the eligible members of a state; typically through elected representatives.

*Educate*—To provide with schooling.

*Equality*—The state of being equal, especially in status, rights, and opportunities.

*Politics*—The activities associated with the governance of a country or other area, especially the debate or conflict among individuals or parties having or hoping to achieve power.

*Psychology*—The science of human behavior.

*Science*—The intellectual and practical activity encompassing the systematic study of the structure and behavior of the physical and natural world through observation and experiment.

*Tabula Rasa*—The theory that at birth the (human) mind is a "blank slate" without rules for processing data, and that data is added and rules for processing are formed solely by one's sensory experiences.

*Zero sum*—A system where in order for one to gain, an equal amount must be removed from another participant; for one to win another has to lose.

**Glossary (LCRWI):**

*At-risk children*—A term that recognizes that childhood itself is a very vulnerable time for all children on earth; a time fraught with uncertain conditions that can prevent children from reaching their full human potential. (The greater the uncertainty, the more at-risk the child is.) In fact, stigmatized children living in societies that do not meet their basic growth and developmental needs (and rights) to food, water, shelter, safety, love, and a quality education, are particularly vulnerable during this time.

*At-risk society*—Any professed democratic social system that stigmatizes some of its children, and does not meet their basic growth and developmental needs (and rights) to food, water, shelter, safety, love, and a quality education—thus preventing them from reaching their full human potential.

*Civic power*—The inalienable right citizens have to determine their own destiny. It includes, but goes beyond the right to vote. That is, it also implies the right of citizens to imagine and work to realize more 'just' systems of democratic power that meet the needs of **all** the people in a society.

*Community education think tank*—A learning community of civically-engaged, emphatic people who have committed themselves to acquiring the knowledge needed to generate scientific and commonsense solutions to the educational challenges facing undervalued *children in the community, and to building educational, research-based institutions to make those solutions last.*

*Culture—As it relates to the human family, culture has both mental and physical properties. At its most critical mental level, culture should be seen as a life-giving and life-sustaining mindset (worldview) that guides and instructs humans on the beliefs and values required to successfully align themselves with governing principles of the natural and spiritual worlds. At the physical level, culture unfolds in laws that govern such human practices as birth, death, food, clothing, labor, capital, art, music, and so on.*

*Educate—To educate means to carry out two fundamental functions: The first is to provide instructions that bring forth in a person pre-existing knowledge and natural gifts-- "inperiential" (an LCRWI word). The second is the inculcation of the necessary societal values (i.e., cultural, economic, moral, civic, etc.) that a person (especially a child) requires to successfully carry out the duties and responsibilities of living in a particular society— "experiential."*

*Public servant—A selfless person who fights for justice, and humbly commits his personal and professional life to serving children, the elderly, the sick, and other vulnerable members of the human family. A public servant follows the strength of his convictions, and listens to his moral conscience. Ideal models: See Harriet Tubman; Nelson Mandela; Malcolm X, and Dr. Martin Luther King, Jr.*

*Responsible democracy—A society where the people have collectively given themselves the power they need to survive, thrive, and generally control their own destiny. Elected and appointed public servants serve at the pleasure of the people, and honor the people's ultimate sovereignty.*

**Suggested Readings:**

- Bame, A Nsamenang. *Human Development in Cultural Context: A Third World Perspective*. Newbury Park. Sage Publication: 1992.

- Bronfenbrenner, U. *The Ecology of Human Development*.
  Massachusetts. Harvard College: 1979

- Day, Carol B. *Faith & Confidence: Positioning our hearts and minds to assure success in the lives of Black children*; "Being Black is Not a Risk Factor: A Strengths-Based Look at the State of the Black Child" NBCDI (2013)

- Fagan, Jay and Glen Palm. *Fathers and Early Childhood Programs*.
  New York, Delmar Learning: 2004

- Hall, Ellen and Jennifer Rudkin. *Seen But Not Heard: Children's Rights in Early Childhood Education*. New York. Teachers College Columbia University Press: 2011

- *Jefferson, Thomas. The Most Important Thing He Ever Wrote: The Declaration of Independence. Retrieved from:*
  <http://www.americaslibrary.gov/aa/jefferson/aa_jefferson_declar_1.html>

- *Kaufman, Michael. Sherelyn R. Kaufman, Elizabeth Chase. Learning Together: The Law, Politics, Economics, Pedagogy, and Neuroscience of Early Childhood Education. Maryland. Rowman & Littlefield: 2015*

- *Knudsen, Eric, James J. Heckman, Judy L. Cameron, and Jack Shonkoff. (2006) Economic, Neurobiological, and Behavioral Perspectives on Building America's Future Workforce." Proceedings of the National Academy of Sciences. USA. July 5; 103(27): 10155-10162. 2006*

- *Locke, John. (1632-1704). An Essay Concerning Human Understanding. New York. Prometheus Books: 1995 (Tabula Rasa)*

- *Spencer, Margaret. "Phenomenological Variant Ecological Systems Theory: Development of Diverse Groups," 2005*
  *"The state of Black America 2014, Redeem the Dream." News & Resources. Marc H. Morial, President and CEO, National Urban League. Accessed April 2014 from Iamempowered.com/soba/home*

*All Children need to be loved!*

*And children who have a history of assault by persons, institutions, and dehumanizing ideas, in particular, need to be loved.*

*-Dr. Stanley Howard*

# Chapter 2

# The Law of Manhood Healing and Empathic Development

**Learning Objective: What is Manhood?**

"The lesson taught at this point by human experience is simply this: that the man who will get up will be helped up and the man who will not get up will be allowed to stay down. Personal independence is a virtue and it is the soul out of which comes the sturdiest manhood. But there can be no independence without a large share of self-dependence, and this virtue cannot be bestowed. It must be developed from within."

**-Frederick Douglass**

The *foundation* of manhood is established at birth, when a male child enters the world. After this, manhood develops and matures when a man chooses to make a commitment to follow the adage: "know thyself" and then dedicates himself to building and sustaining a multi-generational positive support system. By doing so, men, especially those of color, are putting themselves in a strong position to challenge the model of the "ideal American man" that is presented in mainstream media and cultural institutions. Research in the fields of neuroscience and the bio-developmental sciences have identified the following foundational needs that males have at birth and extend into manhood:

- The need to be loved and to show love through nurturing, trusting, caring, and respecting
- The need to build things of value to solve human challenges
- The need to guide and protect the weak from the strong

**He Said…**

The definition of what a man is has been suggested by many. In Gerald Levert's song, "Definition of a Man" he said, "I'll care for you. Be there for you. I'll share with you. I'll understand. I'll be your friend. That's my definition of a man." But does this sum it up? What about the children that are often created by all of that caring and sharing? Men, might I suggest, need to broaden that definition. As a father of four (two boys and two girls) I could have really used this information during my children's developmental stages. Not that it didn't exist; I just wasn't exposed to it at that time. Since raising my consciousness concerning the ways in which children learn best, and how that scientifically and specifically pertains to me, had I been equipped with these tools sooner, I believe it would have helped me be a better man, father, and mentor. Thankfully, I have now started the journey on the road to manhood healing and empathic development. I'm excited to share with you what I'm discovering.

**She Said…**

As women, it is our responsibility to understand the struggles our men face, just by wearing their skin as American citizens. When coupled with their struggle to understand what it means to be an honorable man, we must dig deeper than mere understanding. We must respect and empathize with whom they are and whom they are striving to become. We must let them know, in a positive way, that we understand what they are going through and avail ourselves to them without being pushy or controlling. There is a lot of truth in the saying, "Behind every successful man is a strong woman." Our responsibility is to remember that his success is not defined by his socioeconomic status, but his commitment to elevate his consciousness and mature his empathic system.

**What Do You Think?**

Several questions were asked and answered in the text, but we want to know what you think. Take a moment to contemplate and respond to the following:

1. How do men, i.e., fathers, grandfathers, and uncles, know that children need to be loved?
2. How do we, as parents, know that we are giving our children the love they need?
3. How do most American men measure up to the task of giving children the love they need?
4. What does it mean to be a man? What does it mean to be an American man?
5. If you're a man, do you believe you measure up? If you're a woman, how do you believe men in your life measure up? How and why do you have this belief?

# Chapter 2
## The Law of Manhood Healing and Empathic Development

**Did You Know?**

A man who has not shown a commitment to elevating his consciousness and to maturing his empathic system cannot hear the multitude of voices of children who are yearning for love. That same man, by committing to knowing himself, has made a commitment to know love, and when he knows love, he knows of love's oneness. He knows that it is indivisible, and that as someone who knows love, he is connected to all members of the human family and other living creatures throughout the universe.

**In-Class Activity (TBA):**

**Student Assignments:**

**Readings:**
- Bloom, Paul. *"The Moral Life of Babies," The New York Times Magazine, 2010*
- Howard, Dr. Stanley. *Righting America's Wrongs: A Best Practices Manual For Educating Black Male Youth. (Chapter 2)* Illinois. Law and Civics Publishing: 2014
- *"Persistent Fear and Anxiety Can Affect Young Children's Learning and Development: Working Paper No. 9."*
  *Retrieved from* www.developingchild.harvard.edu *2010*

**Videos:**
- Bailey, Becky. (2011, Nov. 22). *Developing Empathy – Conscious Discipline Skills.*
  http://www.ConsciousDiscipline.com
- CommLab India. (2011, Jun. 17). *Developing Empathic Listening Skills –*
  http://bit.ly/iNLe8a
- Harvard University. *Experiences Build Brain Architecture.*
  https://shar.es/1pQgsH
- Harvard University. *Serve & Return Interaction Shapes Brain Circuitry.*
  https://shar.es/1pQgpy

- Harvard University. *Toxic Stress (Empathy Development).*
  https://shar.es/1pQfLs

**Service Learning Project (Community Field Work):**

Ask two (2) young men (ages 16-25) to name and describe their dating ritual. Then ask two (2) male seniors (over age 55) to define and describe the dating ritual called "courting." Compare and contrast the two courting practices.

_____
_____
_____
_____
_____
_____
_____
_____
_____
_____
_____
_____
_____
_____
_____

**Glossary (General):**

*Empathy—The natural ability to not only put yourself in another person's place, during times of strife, but the willingness to take action.*
*Heal—To make or become healthy, sound or whole. To cure or remedy.*
*Mentor—A wise and trusted counselor or teacher.*
*Prolactin--A hormone that causes sympathetic pregnancy in a father-to-be and increases a father's ability to hear his baby's cry.*

**Glossary (LCRWI):**

*American Man—A man with the inborn qualities of:*
- *Rugged individualism—born self-centered and anti-social.*
- *Hyper-masculinity—born a "pure man," possessing no traces of female biological or social traits.*
- *Retributive justice—born with a vengeful, "eye for an eye" life orientation.*
- *Economic acquisitiveness—born to elevate "manly" status by acquiring more and more material things. Supports an "end justifies the means" and "get rich or die trying" economic value system.*

*Know thyself—To cultivate self-knowledge as the highest practice in acquiring knowledge. In order to know others, one must first know oneself.*

*Male mentoring —The social process of building empathic and trusting relationships between boys and young men seeking non-judgmental life-giving, life-sustaining, and resilience guidance from self-disciplined men in secure possession of this knowledge. At its best, mentoring is rooted in reciprocity, intergenerational relations, and cultural-affirmation.*

*Man—The male member of the human species that commits himself to developing three in-born needs of manhood:*

1. *To Love*
2. *To Guide*
3. *To Work*

**Suggested Readings:**

- *Barbarin, Oscar. (2010) "Halting African American Boys' Progression From Pre-K to Prison: What Families, Schools, and Communities Can Do!"*
  *The Community, American Journal of Orthopsychiatry, vol. 80, No. 1, 81-88*

- Brizendine, Louann. *The Male Brain.* New York, NY. Broadway Books: 2010

- Fagan, Jay and Glen Palm. *Fathers and Early Childhood Programs.*
  New York, Delmar Learning: 2004

- Hooks, bell. *We Real Cool: Black Men and Masculinity.*
  New York, NY. Routledge: 2004

- Johnson, Waldo. *Social Work with African American Males: Health, Mental Health, and Social Policy.* New York, Oxford Press: 2010

- Muhammad, Khalil Gibran. *The Condemnation of Blackness: Race, Crime, and the Making of Modern Urban America.* Massachusetts. Harvard University Press: 2011

- Sprung, Barbara, M. Froschl, and N. Gropper. *Supporting Boys Learning.*
  New York. Teachers College Press: 2010

- Trout, J.D. *The Empathy Gap: Building Bridges to the Good Life and the Good Society.*
  New York. Viking: 2009

*Black leadership and Black men*

*must appreciate more fully*

*that since the beginning of time,*

*child development,*

*economic development, and community development*

*are all inseparably linked to*

*women's health, safety, and well-being.*

*-Dr. Stanley Howard*

# Chapter 3

## The Law of Maternal Health and Well-Being

**Learning Objective: The Impact of Maternal Depression and Stress**

The Law of Maternal Health and Well-Being delivers the message that a society's well-being, future, and survival ultimately rest on the extent to which its women are honored and respected with equality and justice in the areas of health, safety, education, economics, and law. Men must appreciate more fully that since the beginning of time, child development, economic development, and community development are all inseparably linked to women's health, safety, and well-being.

**He Said…**

A good friend of mine always says, "To be aware is to be alive." I agree totally! I'd like to take it further. To be aware of the health and well-being of your woman, especially when she is pregnant with your child, will determine the quality of life that you all live. I know that's wordy, but I believe it's true. It's amazing to me, how deep the damage potentially goes. Based on research at the Institute, the health and well-being of the pregnant mother is inextricably linked to the health and well-being of the child in utero and beyond. There is much that men can do. One thing is to be aware of how a mother's stress levels, if toxic, are not only dangerous to her, but are potentially threatening to the unborn child's brain architecture and its development. Finding ways to reduce her stress and applying them offers positive possibilities for both her and the child. I've heard it said, "Happy wife: happy life." Well, I'll add, "Happy lady: happy baby!"

**She Said...**

In the poem, *The Hand That Rocks the Cradle Is the Hand That Rules the World*, William Ross Wallace celebrates the majesty and divinity that is "mother." And rightfully so, because "mother" brought us here, then she nurtures and cares for us, and puts our needs above hers no matter how her partner or society may treat her. We call her strong. We say she is invincible; unbreakable. She wears the mask and swallows her pain; pushes it down and pushes through. But, what gets lost in all the theatrics is this: a mother's emotional and physical health during pregnancy is undeniably transferred to her unborn child. What she thinks, feels, and experiences has a direct and almost immediate impact on the child. With this understanding, it is imperative that we protect "Momma" during this time of wonder and creation. Prenatal and post-partum depression are real and Black women, more than any other culture of women, suffer these and other forms of depression. It is during this time that she needs her man the most. Just as it is our responsibility (the women dedicated to this work) to support our men, the same is expected of our men. This responsibility goes beyond empathy. There must also be compassion, nurturing, and support (what I also like to call "loving kindness"). You, my brothas, must be the 'Guardians at the Gate' protecting "Momma's" physical and emotional well-being during pregnancy and well past birthing; at all costs. The Black man and woman must protect and love each other so that we can strengthen our lineage and, once again, rule *our* world – the Black community.

**What Do You Think?**

1. Where are the honorable men who are prepared to challenge the status quo in Black communities?
2. How long must Black women be blamed for the conditions (over which they exert no control) that destabilize Black families and communities?
3. If mothers are dying during childbirth, experiencing various forms of depression after delivery, and struggling to cope with stressful situations, how bright is a community's future?

**Did You Know?**

- According to the Center for Disease Control, Black American women have the highest maternal mortality rate in the nation.
- Considerable racial disparities in pregnancy-related mortality exist. From 2006-2009, the pregnancy-related mortality ratios were:
  --11.7 maternal deaths per 100,000 live births for White women
  --17.6 maternal deaths per 100,000 live births for women of other races
  --35.6 maternal deaths per 100,000 live births for Black women
- Babies of more highly stressed or anxious mothers tend to be fussier, more irritable, and perhaps even delayed in their mental and motor development (Howard, pg.59)
- Healthy environments with caring, nurturing, and professional caregivers can enhance a child's brain connections up to 25 percent.

**In-Class Activity (TBA):**

**Student Assignments:**

**Readings:**

- Howard, Dr. Stanley. *Righting America's Wrongs: A Best Practices Manual for Educating Black Male Youth. (Chapter 3)* Illinois. Law and Civics Publishing: 2014
- *"Maternal Depression Can Undermine the Development of Young Children: Working Paper No. 8."*
  http://www.developingchild.harvard.edu (Bio-development). *2009*

**Videos:**

- Bennett, Shoshana. (2014 Mar. 20). *Signs of Prenatal Depression.*
  https://youtube/MWO2mprvMAY
- Ham, Nia. (2013, Sep. 27). *Suffering in Silence: Depression in African American Women and Barriers to Treatment.*
  Retrieved from You Tube
- Harvard University. *Building Adult Capabilities to Improve Child Outcomes: A Theory of Change (Eco-cultural & social/emotional development).*
  https://shar.es/1pDFDf
- Muhammad, Stacey. (2012 May 28). *Out of Our Right Minds: Trauma, Depression, and the Black Woman.*
  https://youtube/9xlmCYScjwc

## THE BRAIN

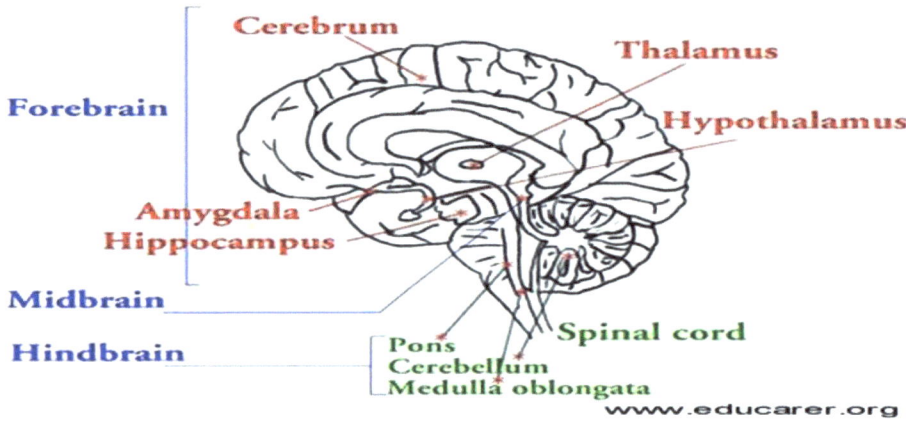

## NEURONS

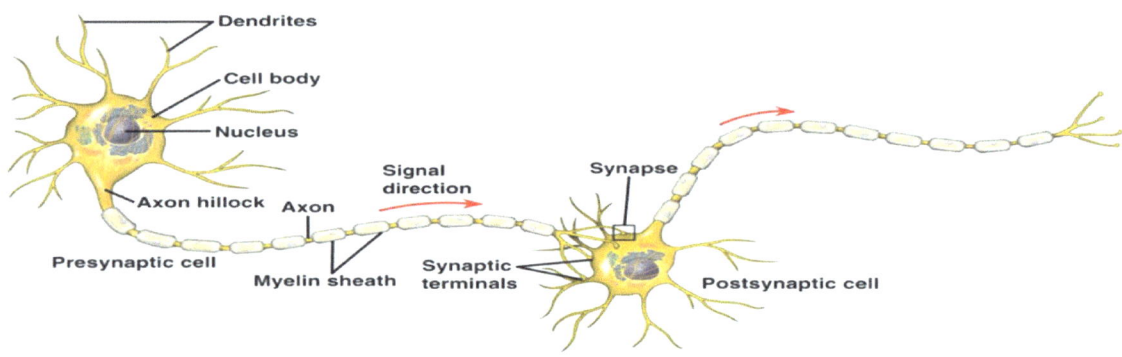

**Service Learning Project (Community Field Work):**

Interview two young women (ages 16-35) in your community and ask them two questions: 1) What are your views on whether you like men who assume a role of "protecting" you? 2) Define what you mean by "protecting?"

**Glossary (General):**

*Brain stem*—The back and lower part of the brain including the midbrain and medulla oblongata.

*Cerebellum*—A large portion of the back part of the brain that is concerned especially with the action of groups of muscles and with bodily balance.

*Gender equality*—Gender equality means that women and men have equal conditions for realizing their full human rights and for contributing to and benefiting from, economic, social, cultural, and political developments. Gender equality starts with the equal valuing of girls and boys.

*Maternal death*—The death of a woman while pregnant or within 42 days of the termination of the pregnancy, irrespective of the duration and site of the pregnancy, from any cause related to or aggravated by the pregnancy or its management, but not from accidental or incidental causes.

*Maternal depression*—Depression that occurs during motherhood, which is a time of increased vulnerability to psychological stress.

*Thalamus*—A subdivision of the forebrain that receives nerve impulses and sends them on to the appropriate parts of the brain cortex.

**Glossary (LCRWI):**

*American External Culture*—As it relates to the educational experiences of Black Americans, this idea acknowledges the systemic impact of the Anglo-American political and economic systems on the low achievement of many Black children; but ultimately sees the solutions to these challenges residing in Black Internal Culture.

*Black Internal Culture*—The idea that in order for Black Americans to produce academically high achieving children, especially children from low-income and no-wealth Black communities, they must first identify, and then dig deeply into the cultural values that they have used historically to both survive and thrive. Afterwards, these historical values must be updated to the 21$^{st}$ century needs and realities within Black communities.

*Eco-Cultural Framework of Development*—Positioning human development research in ecological and cultural contexts.

*Emic Research Approach*—The Emic Research Approach focuses on how local people think; how they perceive and categorize the world; their rules for behavior; what has meaning for them; and how they imagine and explain things.

*Etic Research Approach—The Etic Research Approach shifts the research focus from local observations, categories, explanations, and interpretations to those of the outside observer (e.g. psychologist, anthropologist).*

*Male Empathic Consciousness—The idea that in order to successfully work with Black males in families, schools and communities, men must first tap into and grow their natural empathy.*

*Phenomenological Variant Ecological System Theory--(PVEST) A theory used as a framework to examine strength and resiliency, especially during the process of identity formation, in adolescents. PVEST addresses the social, historical, and cultural context in which youth develop, as well as the perceptions and self-appraisals that individuals use to form their identity.*

**Suggested Readings:**

- "Black Women in the United States, 2014 Progress and Challenges 50 Years After the War on Poverty 50 Years After the 1964 Civil Rights Act 60 Years After Brown v. Board of Education" http://www.washingtonpost.com/r/2010-2019/

- Brizendine, Louann. *The Female Brain.* New York, NY. Broadway Books: 2006

- Cartman, Obari. *"Lady's Man: Conversations For Young Black Men About Relationships and Manhood"* Obari Cartman: 2014

- "Identifying and Treating Maternal Depression: Strategies & Considerations for Health Plans." http://www.nihcm.org/pdf/FINAL_MaternalDepression6-7.pdf

  NIHCM Foundation Issue Brief. June 2010
- Richie, Beth. *Arrested Justice: Black Women, Violence, and America's Prison Nation.* New York. University Press: 2012

*When a society organizes and structures itself*

*in such a way that these needs*

*(to love, to work, to guide, and to protect)*

*are understood, honored, respected,*

*and enshrined in its laws and practices,*

*its men can only flourish.*

*-Dr. Stanley Howard*

## Chapter 4

## The Law of Fathers, 'Surrogate Fathers,' and Honorable Men

**Learning Objective: What is a Father?**

The theory of generative fathering posited by human development psychologist Erick Erickson refers to a commitment to caring for the next generation by working to meet children's needs. According to Erickson, an important part of adult development is enlarging a sense of self to include the next generation (i.e., one's own children and other children) and committing to care for them. He calls this "generativity." Thus, generative fathering is at play when a father raises his consciousness to hear the many voices and cries for love coming from children. In recognizing and acting on these voices, not only does a father make meaningful contributions to a child's development, he also contributes to his own growth and development.

The community in which he lives also reaps great benefits from this decision. Nevertheless, practitioners of the generative fathering approach warn that a commitment to generative fathering involves a great deal of work. Some of the categories of work a father (or surrogate father) commits to by elevating his consciousness through generativity are:
- Relationship work (working to create healthy relationships)
- Stewardship work (providing for the physical needs and safety of children)
- Development work (changing himself to meet changing needs)
- Ethical work (teaching children values and helping them to relate to others in moral ways)

- Spiritual work (working to help children obtain purpose and joy)
- Recreation work (helping children to relax and have fun)
- Mentoring work (helping older children learn the skills necessary to be a successful parent)

**He Said…**

When I looked up the definition of father, I found the simplest description to be "noun—a male parent." Our focus goes beyond this simple description. Another description reads "verb—to act as a father toward; take the responsibility of." It's this action description that aligns more with what we are proposing. I have a great father—a male parent, who took responsibility for me. And as the research shows, I benefited a lot from his presence and protection, his provision and perspectives. But it wasn't until I became a father that I began to realize an additional aspect that the research also indicated. As a father I also benefitted, maybe even as much as my children have, from our interactions.

The other day, I asked a gentleman if he had hope for our future. He said, "No." He began expressing his frustration regarding some recent images of a group of angry young men vandalizing and rioting in the streets. He said, "They (the angry young men) weren't listening." I encouraged him to consider that maybe they're not listening to anyone, because no one is listening to them. Furthermore, maybe they feel hopeless because they see that we are hopeless too.

**She Said…**

I grew up with a single mother who *chose* to raise me—alone. Many single mothers don't get to choose and they also don't get to choose boy or girl. I say, "choose" because as an adoptee, I can say my mother "chose" to raise a girl-child. She was mother and father, teaching me the ways of men, as she knew them to be. However, the absence of a father, or father figure, in my life definitely left an indelible impression and impacted my decisions and choices for a mate. I believe the same rings true for a mother raising a man-child. Sure, she can provide for him. She can keep a roof over his head, clothes on his back, and food in his stomach. She cannot; however, teach him how to be a man and she has to understand and accept this from the outset. She has to know that she cannot successfully raise her son to be an honorable man, which is the ultimate goal, without support. She must employ positive male role models during his early development and they must remain with him throughout his formative years. With this support system, he will learn the responsibilities he has to himself, his community, his family, and the children he will one day bring into the world. He will have a strong sense of self and be committed to care for the next generation. He will make meaningful contributions to his child's development and contribute to his own growth and development.

**What Do You Think?**

- What are you learning and how does this learning relate to fathers and the presence or absence of positive males in early childhood?
- What does nurturing mean to you, and do you believe men/fathers are capable of nurturing their children?
- What do you think of our research into the differences in the male and female brain and how is it relevant to Black male infants, toddlers, and children during early childhood?

**Did You Know?**

Research on the brain development of children suggests that Black boys reap several benefits when fathers and other positive males understand the importance of nurturing and protecting their children's developing brains. These benefits include:
- Greater self-confidence and a motivation to learn
- Higher levels of achievement in school and later in life
- An ability to control aggressive impulses and resolve conflict in nonviolent ways
- The capability of knowing the difference between right and wrong
- A capacity for developing and sustaining casual and intimate relationships
- An example of successful parenting

**In-Class Activity (TBA):**

**Student Assignments:**

**Readings:**
- Howard, Dr. Stanley. *Righting America's Wrongs: A Best Practices Manual For Educating Black Male Youth. (Chapter 4)* Illinois. Law and Civics Publishing: 2014
- *"Young Children Develop in an Environment of Relationships: Working Paper No. 1"* National Scientific Council on the Developing Child, www.developingchild.harvard.edu. (2004)

**Videos:**
- Lammy, David (2010, mar. 15) *Black Fatherhood in the 21st Century* – https://youtube/EtLsET6pKf8
- Van Peebles, Mario. (2014, Feb. 3) *Bringing Your "A" Game* – https://youtube/2Nd4wIGeYUE
- Vanzant, Iyannla. (2014, Oct. 6) *Fix My Life: Fatherhood* – https://youtube/n1wGaOnrvQ8

**Service Learning Project (Community Field Work):**

Bring together an intersection group of three (3) to five (5) Black boys and men, who were raised, or are being raised by a surrogate father. Play the song "Color Him Father" and then engage them in a conversation about the song's meaning and relevance.

**Glossary (General):**

*Father—A male parent.*

*Generative fathering—The commitment of a father to caring for the next generation by working to meet children's needs.*

*The social construction of gender—The view that gender roles (i.e., the behavior of men and women) are socially constructed.*


**Glossary (LCRWI):**

*Father—A male progenitor of an offspring who has tapped into his biological fatherhood energies, as well as his cultural fatherhood values that instruct in the masculine ways of loving, nurturing, caring, guiding, and protecting his offspring and family.*

*Father and Culture-The ideas about what it means to be a committed and involved father varies from culture to culture.*

*Fatherhood Empowerment—Fatherhood programs that navigate fathers through the biological and cultural roots of fatherhood, as well as what they need to know about the political-economic system to protect their needs and rights of being a father.*

*Surrogate father—A man who is not the biological father of a particular child, but nonetheless has chosen to love, nurture, guide, and protect him/her as if he were the biological father.*


**Suggested Readings:**

- Coles, Roberta L. and Charles Green. *The Myth of the Missing Black Father: The Persistence of Black Fatherhood in America,* New York, NY. Columbia Univ. Press: 2010

- Fagan, Jay and Glen Palm. *Fathers and Early Childhood Program.* New York. Delmar Learning:2004

*The child whose mind is respected,*

*protected, and nurtured*

*is easy to identify.*

*He is the happy and active one,*

*eager and excited to explore, learn and,*

*above all else, solve problems.*

*-Dr. Stanley Howard*

# Chapter 5

# The Law of Social, Emotional, and Cognitive Development and Learning

**Learning Objective: Understanding learned "victimization"**

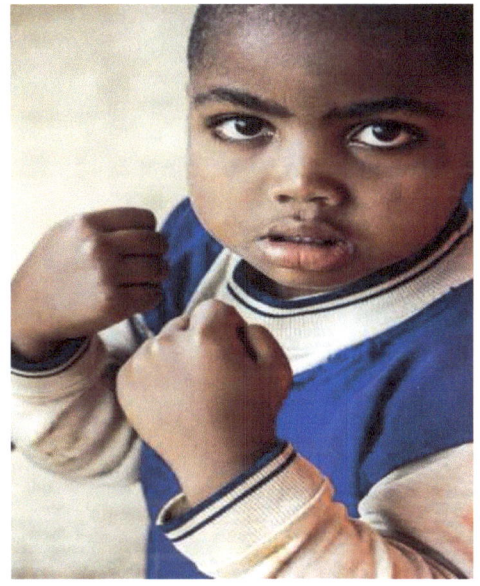

When parents, schools, teachers, and communities stigmatize a Black male child as a "bad boy" or "problem child"; or do not realize that many boys are active learners and need movement in and out of the classroom; or when boys are deprived of the opportunity to play and learn with nature; or are disproportionately discarded into special education classrooms and given behavioral modifying drugs for 'bad' behavior; or when adults refuse to allow them to know and tell their cultural stories, because they are seen as culturally deficient, our society is planting seeds of learned helplessness in that child's mind.

**He Said...**

Playing the dozens, signifying, or cracking on each other is common place in my culture. Talking about somebody's shoes, their house, or even their Mama was what it was, and what you had to get used to. I don't know how many of us ever really got used to it though. How children are socialized leaves them feeling some kind of way. The emotional state they find themselves in, directly affects their ability to think and subsequently determines how they will behave. This is why it is so important to understand how children learn. A professor in a workshop on the brain taught us, "There can be no deep learning without emotion." Regardless of what emotion one may be dealing with at the moment, some deep learning is probably taking place. We have much to learn about this subject, so we can do a better job protecting our children's social, emotional, and cognitive development. If you want a different harvest, you must sow different seed.

**She Said…**

From my first day of kindergarten all the way through high school, I was always the tallest girl in class. I also happened to possess lips that were like a target on my face. My proverbial 'kitchen' stayed dirty and even with a perm, my hair didn't hang past my shoulders. And, add to that, my name was as different as could be and could be morphed into a variety of hurtful words…I was a virtual smorgasbord filled with options for 'playing the dozens.' Luckily for me, I went to predominantly white schools for most of my formative years, and while the kids may have poked fun at my name, they left the rest of me alone. But, whenever I was around Black children (including my own relatives), I got a healthy dose of the 'dozens,' so much so, I'm amazed I survived with most of my self-esteem intact. Fortunately, I was able to do this because my mother taught me to be proud of the parts of me that made me different. She forced me to stand up straight. She gave me numerous ribbings about my lips and helped me to understand that if I could laugh at myself, it would make it harder for me to be bothered when the kids teased me. She told me that all hair was "good" if it grew--short of that, hair was hair. In keeping in line with the rule of thought that "there can be no deep learning without emotion," it is our responsibility to help protect our children's social, emotional, and cognitive development. If we define a child as being "bad," we've already charted their course for the future.

**What Do You Think?**

- What do the issues of curiosity and problem solving have to do with the education of Black males in early childhood?
- Does Black leadership and the nation fail to respect the scientific minds of Black children? What roles do American schools play in this drama?
- What conditions in a child's life lead to stability and strength; rather than deviance?

**In-Class Activity (TBA):**

**Did You Know?**

- As it relates to children, resilience is instilling in a child the belief that: 'I can perform. I have support. And I will accomplish goals whenever confronted with difficult circumstances.'
- When children in early childhood are not honored, respected, nurtured, and protected at home, at school, and in their community, a high likelihood exists that their resilience will be negatively affected.
- A child's capacity for empathy is threatened when their sense of trust is compromised.
- Science reveals that early exposure to circumstances that produce persistent fear and chronic anxiety can have lifelong consequences by disrupting the developing architecture of the brain.

**Student Assignments:**

**Readings:**
- "*Children's Emotional Development Is Built into the Architecture of Their Brains: Working PaperNo.2.*" National Scientific Council on the Developing Child www.developingchild.harvard.edu. (2004)
- Howard, Dr. Stanley. *Righting America's Wrongs: A Best Practices Manual For Educating Black Male Youth. (Chapter 5)* Illinois. Law and Civics Publishing: 2014
- Hughes, Langston. *"Mother to Son"* (1922). The International Resilience Project – Grotberg, Edith H. Ph.D. Senior Scientist Civitan International Research Center, UAB
- Yang-Immordino, M. H. and Antonio Damasio. "*We Feel, Therefore We Learn: The Relevance of Affective and Social Neuroscience to Education.*" Mind, Brain, and Education, 1: 1, 3–10. doi: 10.1111/j.1751-228X.2007.00004.x (2007)

**Videos:**
- Center on the Developing Child-Harvard University (2011, Jan. 6). *InBrief: The Science of Early Childhood Development.*
https://youtube/WO-CB2nsqTA
- Immordino-Yang, Mary Helen. (2011, Feb. 24).
https://youtube/Uad28r_9TPI

**Service Learning Project (Community Field Work):**

Ask four (4) children between the ages of 5-10 (preferably 2 girls and 2 boys) how they feel when others call them derogatory names. Also, ask four (4) adolescent children between the ages of 11-16 (preferably 2 girls and 2 boys) the same question. Then conclude by asking all of them if they felt empowered or victimized by the name calling. Observe and pay close attention to their body language while getting their responses.

## Glossary (General):

*Amygdala (A-mee-g-da-la)*—The emotional center of the human brain. It regulates such emotions as fear.

*Brain stem*—The oldest and deepest area of the brain. It is where vital body functions, such as the heartbeat, respiration, body temperature, and digestion are monitored and controlled.

*Corpus callosum*—The great band of commissural fibers uniting the cerebral hemispheres.

*Hippocampus*—The memory center of the human brain. Converts information from working memory to long-term memory.

*Hypothalamus*—A part of the brain that lies beneath the thalamus and produces hormones which pass to the front part of the pituitary gland, and is important in regulating the activities of the autonomic nervous system.

*Medulla oblongata*—The somewhat pyramid-shaped bottom part of the vertebrate brain that joins the spinal cord and is concerned with the control of involuntary activities necessary for life (such as the heart beat and breathing).

*Prefrontal Cortex*—The higher thinking brain that controls the "Executive" (major decision making) functions of the brain.

## Glossary (LCRWI):

*Boy-friendly learning activities*—The research-based view that many boys (not all) are active learners, and that their learning and behaviors improve when this fact is honored and respected.

*The child's scientific mind*—The research-based proposition that all children are born with curiosity, imagination, and creativity for solving natural and social problems.

*The learned helplessness child mind*—As it relates to Black males in early childhood, the idea that learning activities that are not culturally-responsive, boy-friendly, brain-compatible, and based in nature exploration, create helpless mindsets as opposed to resilient mindsets in these children.

## Suggested Readings:

- Gopnik, Alison. *The Scientist in the Crib.* New York. HarperCollins:1999
- Hakim, Rashid M. "From Brilliant Baby to Child Placed at Risk: The Perilous Path of African American Boys in Early Childhood Education."
  *Journal of Negro Education, 2009*
- "The Timing and Quality of Early Experiences Combine to Shape Brain Architecture: Working Paper No. 5."
  *National Scientific Council on the Developing Child*
  *www.developingchild.harvard.edu* 2007

*The Law of the Rights of Black Males contends*

*that if the nation is to successfully solve*

*the many challenges facing Black males*

*in early childhood and beyond,*

*all Americans, and especially Black men,*

*must come to know America's civic stories,*

*and how these stories affect*

*the life chances of at-risk Black male children.*

*-Dr. Stanley Howard*

# Chapter 6

# The Law of the Rights of Black Male Children

**Learning Objective: The Civil Rights Movement vs. the Human Rights Fight**

If the nation is to successfully solve the many challenges facing Black males in early childhood and beyond, all Americans, and especially Black men, must come to know America's civic stories, and how these stories affect the life-chances of at-risk Black male children. Once they become familiar with these stories, they must then commit themselves to protecting the civil and human rights of these children that are routinely violated by such conditions as the cradle-to-prison pipeline; school suspensions and expulsions; special education referrals; and the mass incarceration of Black males.

**He Said...**

This chapter reminds me of two pieces of literature that I believe would serve us well to read and understand. The first is Chancellor Williams' classic, *The Destruction of Black Civilization*. In the introduction of this work, there is a conversation between a young man and an elder. The young man asked the elder what happened to the people of Sumer; an ancient and great Black civilization. The elder told him, "They forgot their history so they died." In other words, the civic stories weren't told and shared with the youth, so they forgot their history and they died.

The second is in the Bible. In Judges 2:7-11, the story is told of Joshua (Moses' successor) and how his *"...people served the Lord all the days of Joshua and all the days of the elders who outlived Joshua, who had seen all the great works that the Lord did for Israel."* The Bible goes on to say, *"...and there arose another generation after them, which knew not the Lord, nor yet the works which he had done for Israel. And the children of Israel did evil in the sight of the Lord, and served Baalim."* It seems to me that when "any culture" neglects to share its civic stories with its children, destruction seems to follow. That's why our children need to have their civic stories told to them; so they can develop the resilience and confidence that they will acquire when they are so informed. The confidence and resilience to solve their own problems produce a healthy and hopeful attitude about their lives. This chapter demonstrates how our children learn and obtain an understanding of their value as we effectively connect them to their civic stories.

### She Said...

"To be armed is to be forewarned." These were words that my mother shared with me on a regular basis while I was growing up. At the time, these felt like big words and didn't make much sense. I can now say, as I look back, being proud of who I am as a Black girl (and now a Black woman), the saying helped me be forewarned as to what I should expect from society. In school I was taught that the only contribution my ancestors made to civilization was through servitude and suffering. When I went home, my mother taught me that we contributed much more than these futile and disparaging attributes. We were the founders of civilization; possessing skills and talents that we did not receive credit for, but rather were attributed to the Greeks and Romans. There's a saying, "If you do not know where you come from, then you don't know where you are, and if you don't know where you are, then you don't know where you're going. And if you don't know where you're going, you're probably going wrong." Helping our children understand that they are not survivors of or even representations of "down-trodden victims of society," but they are the descendants of the creators of civilization. This will do volumes to help them understand their value and connect them to their civic and human responsibilities.

### What Do You Think?
- If our civil rights leaders had not been gunned down in the prime of their lives, can you image what the Black community and America would be today?

### In-Class Activity (TBA):

**Did You Know?**

- In the Universal Declaration of Human Rights, the United Nations has proclaimed that childhood is entitled to special care and assistance.
- According to the First Amendment (paraphrased), "You can think what you want, and say what you think."
- Dr. King and other leaders are quoted as saying that one of the primary goals of the Civil Rights Movement was to boldly assert a more accurate view of Black humanity, culture, and civilization.

**Student Assignments:**

**Readings:**

- Howard, Dr. Stanley. *Righting America's Wrongs: A Best Practices Manual For Educating Black Male Youth. (Chapter 6)* Illinois. Law and Civics Publishing: 2014
- "Supportive Relationships and Active Skill-Building Strengthen the Foundations of Resilience: Working Paper 13."
  *Center on the Developing Child at Harvard University.*
  *www.developingchild.harvard.edu (2015)*

**Videos:**

- Harvard University. *Building Adult Capabilities to Improve Child Outcomes: A Theory of Change.*
  https://shar.es/1pDFDf
- wviadvocacy. (2014, Mar.7).
  *Listening to Children's Voices.*
  https://youtube/8BGTBuIDh6U

**Service Learning Project (Community Field Work):**

Ask a group of teenaged boys and girls, whether they believe the music that they listen to accurately portrays their civic stories. If so, have them provide you with the names of the songs that do so. If not, ask them how they feel about this music and the messages it delivers to them.

_____
_____
_____
_____
_____
_____
_____
_____
_____
_____
_____
_____
_____
_____
_____
_____
_____
_____
_____
_____
_____
_____
_____
_____
_____
_____
_____
_____

**Glossary (General):**

*Civil Rights Movement*—A social movement, whose goals were to end racial segregation and discrimination against Black Americans and to secure legal recognition and federal protection of the citizenship rights enumerated in the Constitution and federal law.

*Freedom of expression*—The ability to express one's ideas, emotions, and or thoughts, openly without fear.

*Freedom of thought*—The ability to be curious, imaginative, and creative without filters or censorship.

*UN Convention on the Rights of a Child (UNCRC)*—A human rights treaty, which sets out the civil, political, economic, social, health and cultural rights of children.

**Glossary (LCRWI):**

*Children Civic Heart Story ("Taming the Wilderness")* —The official story of the beginning of the American republic. It is a story of heroism, tremendous sacrifice, and great suffering. This authoritative story is intended to attach the most cherished American children to the American political economy, and instill in them a sense of pride and patriotism. It is especially directed to White children in the upper stratum of American society.

*Children Civic Heart and Mind Story*—This story challenges the "civic heart" story by offering a more inclusive and accurate picture of the creation of the American republic. It is a factual and continuing story of how various excluded groups struggled to give real meaning to the civic terms of democracy, equality, justice, and freedom. This story is intended to provide <u>all children</u> in pluralist America a true "We the People" picture of American civic history.

**Suggested Readings:**

- Alexander, Michelle. *The New Jim Crow*. New York, NY. The New Press: 2012

- Articles of the *United Nations Convention and the Rights of the Child* (Appendix) *Righting America's Wrongs*: (pgs. 164-165).

- Hall, Ellen and Jennifer Rudkin. *Seen and Heard: Children's Rights in Early Childhood Education* – London, Ontario. Althouse Press: 2011

- Harding, V. *Hope and History: Why we must Share the Stories of The Movement*. Maryknoll, N.Y. Orbis Books: 1990.

*What Black children need is an educational philosophy*

*that defines the term "quality education"*

*as being rooted in moral responsibility*

*and scientific preparation*

*and that honors and respects*

*their rights to express their curiosity,*

*to exercise their imagination and creativity,*

*and use their critical thinking abilities.*

*-Dr. Stanley Howard*

## Chapter 7

## What is a Quality Education?

**Learning Objective: The Quality Education…what does it look like? Can it ever exist?**

An educational philosophy and practice grounded in 'what to think' as opposed to 'how to think,' limits a child's imagination, moral development, intellectual development, and even business reach. Moreover, the value of an education that teaches children how to think is reflected in the work of education futurists, who tell us that the global economic realities of the twenty-first century will increasingly demand that our children know how to learn on their own, a consequence that occurs only when we first honor and respect their curious, imaginative, creative, and critically thinking mind—a mind possessing multiple intelligences, that must be measured with multiple assessment tools.

**He Said…**

When all of the stakeholders in our democratic society understand and realize that we all have the responsibility and should be committed to the moral and scientific development of the minds of our children, and particularly, those from low-income, no-wealth and culturally-struggling urban and rural communities, we will then be demonstratively closer to what a "Quality Education" looks like. Is the ultimate goal of education to teach students 'what to think,' so that they might become better low-level workers in a twenty-first century economy; or is it to teach them 'how to think,' so they may come to know the vast human, moral, and scientific possibilities that emerge when schools develop a child's natural curiosity, imagination, and creativity?

**She Said…**

The question of a quality education should have been asked and answered when Brown won the legal battle with the Board of Education. It's clear, then and now, that the 'powers that be' decided they would give us entry to the brick and mortar of the white education system, but continue to deny us the access to the content of said system. We could continue banging our heads against that proverbial brick wall insisting that our children deserve access, but if we stepped back for a moment, we would see that the demand needs to be reshaped. No. We don't just want our children to have access to an educational system that's designed to dumb us down. We want access to a world-class education. What does that mean? It means we want our children to effectively compete with Chinese, African, South Korean, Canadian, and upper crust American children. Period! Hard stop! What does a world-class education look like? Well, that's for us to ask and answer, once and for all. And we will.

**What Do You Think?**
- Is the ultimate goal of education to teach students 'what to think,' so that they might become better low level workers in a twenty-first century economy; or is it to teach them 'how to think;' so they may come to know the vast human, moral, and scientific possibilities that emerge when schools develop a child's natural curiosity, imagination, and creativity?
- What role does early childhood education play in the academic and behavioral problems so evident in many Black males during puberty and adolescence?

**In-Class Activity (TBA):**

**Did You Know?**
- Only three (3) out of every 100 Black males entering kindergarten will graduate from college.
- Only 10 percent of eighth-grade Black boys, in public schools across America, read at or above a proficient level.
- Black male preschoolers have the highest rate of expulsions over any other ethnic or racial group.
- There are more Black men in prison today than there were during periods of American chattel slavery in the mid-eighteenth century in America.

**Student Assignments:**

**Readings:**
- Howard, Dr. Stanley. *Righting America's Wrongs: A Best Practices Manual For Educating Black Male Youth. (Chapter 7)* Illinois. Law and Civics Publishing: 2014
- National Scientific Council on the Developing Child (2007). *The Timing and Quality of Early Experiences Combine to Shape Brain Architecture:* Working Paper No. 5. Retrieved from www.developingchild.harvard.edu

## Culminating Personal and Group Community Service Project:
## Early Childhood Demonstration Center

Based on the scientific and commonsense information you have received from the course, your final assignment is in the area of service learning (community fieldwork). In this chapter, you are asked to make a contribution as a citizen, and community of citizens, committed to the 'whole child' education of vulnerable children living in toxic American environments. More specifically, you are asked to gather community research data in order to build a child development model (plan) that will facilitate the creation of solution-based education think tanks that are seamlessly connected to high-quality pre-kindergarten through eighth grade community schools. As an individual and a group, your plan should address the following research-grounded subjects:

1. Cite and discuss two reasons why solution-based education think tanks created on ecological and cultural development principles might close the achievement gap of children of color living in low-resourced and underserved communities in the United States.
2. What is the optimal civic climate needed to realize such a project?
3. Rank the top three (3) development theories that make the best case for a solution-based education think tank to assist in the development and learning of undervalued children in general, and Black boys in particular.
4. What concrete role must community stakeholders/guardians play in this process? **Focus your response on tangible goals and objectives.**

5. Develop a questionnaire with five (5) questions that community stakeholders/guardians must answer before an education think tank can be realized? Administer the questionnaire to five (5) young parents living in your community.
6. Finally, from start to completion, how would you measure how well your plan is proceeding, and how will you sustain its success once achieved?

After you have developed your personal plan by answering these questions, come together as a group to discuss and analyze the strengths and weaknesses of each individual plan, using the questions/statements above as your format. After analyzing the individual plans, distill the consensus from each into a collective plan. Finally, as a group, you will present this collective plan to the class.

Note: You are required to submit written copies of both your personal and collective plans.

**Format:**

- ✓ Personal Plan (3-pages, typed double spaced)
- ✓ Collective Plan (5-pages, typed double spaced)

**Suggested Readings:**

- "Increasing the Achievement of African American Males. Department of Research, Evaluation, and Assessment." *Research Brief, No. 3. Virginia Beach City Public Schools. Ahead of the Curve: 2009*
- Willis, Judy. *Research-Based Strategies to Ignite Student Learning: Insights from a Neurologist and Classroom Teacher.* ASCD: 2006

# Course Evaluation

**Overall**

- Overall, how successful would you consider this class? Please include a brief comment or explanation.

**Content**

- How well did the class meet its articulated goals and objectives?
- What was most revealing to you about development theory and educating children of color?
- How will you apply what you learned in this class?
- How will you apply what you have learned in the service learning part of the class?
- What professional support will you need to implement what you have learned in this course?
- How relevant were the topics to your personal and professional life?
- How well did the topics explored in this course meet a specific need under your job responsibilities?

**Process**

- How well did the instructional techniques and activities facilitate your understanding of the topic?
- How can you incorporate the activities into your daily personal and professional life; beginning today?
- Was any particular activity memorable? What made it stand out?

**Context**

- Was the facility conducive to learning?
- Were the classroom accommodations adequate for the activities in which you were engaged?

Source: Adapted from *"How the Special Needs Brain Learns"*, David Sousa, Corwin Press. 2007.

www.ingramcontent.com/pod-product-compliance
Lightning Source LLC
Chambersburg PA
CBHW041124300426
44113CB00002B/55